1-75

NEW WAY

EASY S

CW01045740

Sweets

Written by Keith Gaines

Illustrated by Margaret de Souza

Nelson

Yum, yum, sweets,
said Rob.
Please can I have some sweets.

No,
said Mum.
Sweets are not good for you.

Eggs are good for you,
said Mum.
Go and get some eggs, please.

Rob took the eggs and
put them in the basket.

Yum, yum, cakes,
said Rob.
Please, **please** can I have a cake.

No,

said Mum.

Cakes are not good for you.

Nuts are good for you.

Go and get some nuts, please.

Rob took the nuts and
put them in the basket.

Yum, yum, lemonade,
said Rob.
Please, **please, please**
can I have some lemonade.

No,
said Mum.
Lemonade is not good for you.

Milk is good for you.

Go and get some milk, please.

Rob took the milk and
put it in the basket.

Yum, yum, buns,
said Rob.
Please, **please, please, please**
can I have a bun.

No,
said Mum.
Buns are not good for you.
Do you want a book?

Yes please,
said Rob.

I will have **this** book.